Love Among The Ruins

DAN M. KHANNA

Copyright © 2015 Dan M. Khanna

All rights reserved.

ISBN: 0692374930
ISBN-13: 978-0692374931

DEDICATION

To Allison, my wife and beloved

Who completes me as a human.

CONTENTS

Prologue

Part 1 - Then	1
Love Among the Ruins	2
The Hopeless Romantic	3
The Broken Heart	4
The End of an Affair	5
Broken Heart	6
The Illusion of Happiness	8
Love is a Razor's Edge	9
The Curse of the Romantic	10
The Bleeding Stone	12
Love is a Mirage	13
The End of an Affair (2)	14
The Wounds of Love	15
The Dangling Hope	16
The Illusion of Love	17
The Love Life	18
The Love of Life	19
Without Love	20
Part 2 - Now	21
Love Among the Ruins (2)	22
Love of My Life	23
My Anchor	25
The Presence	26
Love is Forever	27
By My Side	28
My Love	29
The Love of My Life	30
The Love Feast	31
The Feast of Love	36
The World in My Arms	43
The Passion	44
The Touch	45

The Sheets	46
I Remember You	50
Contentment	51
The Moment	52
Yes, I Love You	53
Together Yet Apart	54
The Empty Bed	55
The Love of My Life (2)	56
Together Yet Alone	57

PROLOGUE

"When love beckons to you, follow him,

Though his ways are hard and steep.

And when his wings enfold you, yield to

Him,…

Love gives naught but itself and takes

naught but from itself.

Love possesses not nor would it be

Possessed;

For love is sufficient unto love."

<u>The Prophet</u>

Kahlil Gibran

PART 1

THEN

LOVE AMONG THE RUINS

The ruins
Of an ancient civilization
Are the best places
For love
Just like
A radiant flower
In the wilderness
Beautifies the forest
Love blossoms
The lonely life
Even if it does
For a short time
It gives life
To a dead soul
Love is,
And should remain,
Among the ruins.

THE HOPELESS ROMANTIC

I love romance
Even though I don't have it
The giddy feeling
The butterflies
Staring into each other's eyes
Moist and tender
Holding hands
The gentle touch
Sharing hopes and dreams
Of a new future
Where we are one
In a world
Of our creation
Full of love and happiness.

It may be a dream
But it feels good
To think of romance
And be in love
Even if it is not there
It is me
The hopeless romantic.

THE BROKEN HEART

The broken heart
Is a precious ornament
That should hang
From the top of the tallest tree
Radiating love
With brilliant colors
That spread
Throughout the universe
It is a heart
That knows love
That loves
Does not worry
About the consequences
It followed its heart
It wanted to love
Love is eternal
It felt the pang
It felt the pain
It is seasoned
Cultured
Experienced
It is a heart
That grows
That grows into a
Beautiful tree
That gives
Shade, fruits and flowers
Beautifies the world
And plants seeds
For new trees
Love it
Cherish it
The broken heart.

THE END OF AN AFFAIR

The end of an affair
Is an occasion
To celebrate
Love
For you loved
You were able to love
That is a gift
But, that does not mean
That love finds happiness
Maybe, it is not meant to be
It is over
You are richer
You are loved
Love resides in you
The affair may be over
But love remains
In you.

BROKEN HEART

A broken heart
Is a rich heart
Full of experiences
Of happiness and sorrow
It knows the pleasure
It knows the pain
It is a happy heart
That is full of memories of love
It once had
And it once cherished
It is a proud heart
That knew how to love
How to feel the emotions
Of joy and completeness
It did not ask how it will end
For heart is pure emotion
That thrives on love
Seeking its pleasure
And worried about pain
But, it does get broken
It is okay
It may never be complete
It may never be new
But, it is wiser
More contemplative
More experienced
More seasoned
It is an ancient tree
That has withstood
The onslaughts of seasons
But still stands erect

Just like my heart
Broken, but tall
Damaged but strong
For it is my heart.

THE ILLUSION OF HAPPINESS

The illusion of happiness
Is a dangerous mirage
That feels like an oasis
Yet it is a barren desert
Ready to swallow you
In its quicksand
While you cling
To an image of
Paradise
That exists only
In your mind
While the reality hits you
Like a jackhammer
Bringing you to your senses
That happiness is just a dream
It does happen
When it does
But mostly
Happiness is just an illusion.

LOVE IS A RAZOR'S EDGE

Love is a razor's edge

A sharp line
that divides
hurt from happiness.

Walking that line
is itself painful.

Yet from that pain
may come some pleasure.

Pain and pleasure
do exist
side by side
Each having
its own joy

Just like love
on the razor's edge.

THE CURSE OF THE ROMANTIC

I am romantic
I love romance
I want to love
Experience the feeling
The butterfly youth
I am ready to endure
And the pain that may come with it
But the joy
When you find love
Overshadows the hurt
But romance is an illusion
That reality shatters
For romance is a curse
It only brings expectations
Desires that remain unfulfilled
But still remain
Tug of war
Being pulled in two directions
Pulling you apart
Tormenting with pain
That spreads through you
Sending jolts of lightening
Through your body
You can't laugh
You can't cry
Laughter is hurting
Tears are stones
That just stay there
Romance is a curse
You want it
You don't want it
That is the paradox

You live with the duality
An eternal struggle
That remains with you
'Til you die
That is the curse of the romantic.

THE BLEEDING STONE

The stone
That bleeds tears
Is my heart
A pulsating emotion
That crashed into a meteorite
Instantly turning into a molten stone
That bleeds at will
As it gets kicked and thrown
To fall with pain
On a cruel surface
Shrieking a silent scream
That no one hears
It sits alone
Waiting for the next kick
Waiting for someone
To pick up
And throw far away
To be picked up again
Maybe, the stone is unique
It has a personality
That someone will hold it
Caress it
And take it
For a collector item
To sit alone
Among other stones
Reflecting how it got there
Bleeding tears
Of joy and sorrow
Staying still
In perpetual stillness
To be forgotten forever.

LOVE IS A MIRAGE

Love is a mirage
I see it
It is far
It is near
I will reach it
Touch it
And embrace it
And quench myself
In its sweetness
I move towards it
It moves further
I run
It runs
The faster I move
The faster it moves
I get tired
I can see it
But cannot touch it
It is there
But not there
Love is
Just like a mirage

THE END OF AN AFFAIR

It was great
While it lasted
Yes, it did have its moments
Pleasure and pain
Both exciting sensations
That grinds you in ecstasy
To propel you to the end of an affair
Full of memories
Both good and bad
Leaving us rich
In experiences and wisdom
To face the next affair
With dignity.

THE WOUNDS OF LOVE

The wounds of love
Are precious
They should be
Nurtured
And treated with
Love and tenderness
For these wounds are
Divine
A gift of God
That tells us
That we can love
And we are not
Afraid to get hurt
The feeling of love
Is God
Cherish it
Respect it
And thank God
For having it.

THE DANGLING HOPE

The hope is still there
For a life
Of romance and passion
To love someone special
Who loves you freely
To hold each other
'Til our bodies and soul
Merge into one
Such that we move in unison
To the rhythms of
Life and living
With a passion
That invigorates and ignites
Desires
To live in a world
That is so special
Full of love and contentment
Peaceful existence
In the bosom of life

THE ILLUSION OF LOVE

Love
Is it real
Or is it an illusion
That exists only in our minds
The reality and illusion
Are one and the same
For they both cause emotions
That we cannot control
Emotions that run us
Makes us feel things
That we don't want to feel
For that feeling
Clouds our thinking
And makes us do things
That we may regret
For love creates an illusion
That all will work out
And will be well
And happiness will prevail
And that is an illusion
The illusion of love

THE LOVE LIFE

The love life!
What is it?
A life of love
Or, love of life.
I like life
But, do I love it?
Do I have to?
I did not choose my life
So, why should I love it?
But, then since I am in life
It is my life
I must love it
Why?
But, I can love
I can love life
If I want to
For loving is good
It feels good
But, it will be better
If I had a love
A love I could love
To make it
A real love life
A life of love
With the love of your life
Then you can love life
And life loves you
And that is
A love life.

THE LOVE OF LIFE

The love of life
Is a gift
Given by God
That propels you
To accept life
As divine
With a purpose
To make it
The way you want to
Some do some don't
Is that destiny?
Life is love
Love it
For it is yours
You have to live it
Love your life
And live with
Passion and virtue
For you are love.

WITHOUT LOVE

Without love
Life could be simple
But not worth living
It would be painless
But not pleasurable
I may be happy
And alone
But not contented
And full
It will be life
Just an ordinary life
Not a life
Worth living
Life
Without love.

PART 2

NOW

LOVE AMONG THE RUINS

Love among the ruins
Can blossom the wilderness
Into an oasis
Of beauty and splendor
The same ruins
That lay desolate and lonely
Without love
Become a garden
Of colorful flowers
Scent and aroma
Abound of intoxicating feelings
Exciting adventures begin

That take us
Into journeys across
Different artful places
Into a world
Where it is just love
Just us
And then those ruins
No longer matter
For love can happen anywhere
Even in the ruins.

LOVE OF MY LIFE

The first time
I saw you
You wore green
Slim and elegant
With flowing hair
Long, soft and gentle
Our ride was smooth
The dinner was delicious
A gentle touch
The rubbing of legs
Exciting feelings
Of longing
The talk
Touching of hands
Not letting it go
The sweet smell
Of lips
That reached for each other
It just happened
The caressing of lips
The sweet smell of tongues
Passed an electricity
That told us
That we are in love
We are one
The quiet embrace
The flowing of emotions
Letting life
Guide us
Plunging us
In the hands of God
To hold
And tie our souls

Into one soul
The united soul
The love of my life
Which you are
And will remain
Forever.

MY ANCHOR

The ship
Has an anchor
It lowers
To stabilize
We as humans
Need an anchor
That keeps us
On track of life.

I have an anchor,
My beloved,
That holds me in place
Stabilizes me
So I don't
Wander in wayward seas
She keeps me
In a direction
That is calm, gentle and soothing
I am at peace
With the world and myself
The reward of emotional stability
She is there
Solid as steel
With a gentle embrace
That holds me to me
Protects me from myself
And keeps me in place
She is my anchor
She is my beloved.

THE PRESENCE

The presence
Is a feeling
That tells me
You are near
Even when you are far
I feel you
Your touch
Your sensation
Your thoughts
From a distance
Physical is an illusion
Presence is felt
When thoughts feel
It is a feeling
That stays with you
All the time
'Til death
That you are with me
Beyond life
Always present.

LOVE IS FOREVER

My love for you
Transgresses eternity
Into a time
That has no ending
It transports
Into many lifetimes
Where our souls are intermingled
Into one body
That travels together
Into space
Through heavenly bodies
Seeing colors and visions
That only we share
Only we experience
The journey is forever
It never ends
It goes on
To the heart of God
For our love
Is immortal
Is forever.

BY MY SIDE

By my side
Is that side
That is all around me
It is not just one side
But it is all sides
Around me
Where you are
On all my sides
Touching me
Feeling me
At all angles
At all ends
There is then
No side
Just you and me
Without sides
Immersed in each other
When all sides disappear
And we are just one
Without a side.

MY LOVE

You are my love
My one and only love
From the first time I saw you
I knew I was in love
Love, a feeling
That emerges from within
To engulf mind and body.

I knew I was in love
When you brushed against me
When you touched me
It was electric
It was natural
As if our bodies were
Made for each other
Then we kissed
And our love was complete
The kiss
The touch
The holding
Our bodies and minds
Intertwined with love and emotions
Embracing a future
That was going to be ours
A future
Where love is pure
And everlasting
And two bodies and souls
Become one
To journey together
In the heart of God
To be one soul.
You are my love.
You are my soul.

THE LOVE OF MY LIFE

The love of my life
Has moist lips
Gentle hands
Tender touch
And a smile
That brightens my life.

The love of my life
Holds me together
In her warm embrace
With searching touches
That caress
The emotions
To make me come alive.

The love of my life
Kisses me
With quivering lips
Igniting passion
That envelops
The entire body
And makes me whole.

The love of my life
Loves me
With yielding passion
Probing depths
That are unreachable
Exploring emotions
And unleashing feelings
That could swallow
The entire universe.

THE LOVE FEAST

The last night
We were together
Was a night to remember
Engraved in our memories
Forever

It was a night
When love blossomed
Passions bloomed
Senses peaked
Bodies
Gorged on each other
Feasting with pleasure
Each other's flesh
Devouring skin
Exploring each orifice
To savor
Every delight
To taste
Every scent

It was
The feast of love
Tasting
Every sensuous sensation
Every quiver of the flesh
Nothing was enough
The night would last forever
The lips locked
In sweet embrace
Sucking sweet nectar.

The tongues
Intertwined with each other
Making passionate love
Pushing, pulling and sucking.
Trying to plunge
Into the soul.

The hands
The tongue
Caressing the body
Gently and firmly
Spreading all over
Feeling each wave
Skin
Cupping the breast
In loving embrace
'Til the hardness of nipples
Invited the mouth
To suck like a baby
Thirsty for milk
To flow out of the breast
Into the thirsty mouth
As your hands
Explore the hardness
That is ready
To erupt
Like a volcano
Ready to squirt
Its hot juices
All over your body.

But the feast has just begun
As bodies
Hungrily attack each other

Sucking life out of
Every orifice
Every hole
'Til there is nothing else to eat
The lips sucking
Every sweetness
From your nest
While your lips
Gently suck
Every part of my body.

'Til there is nothing else
To eat
And then we plunge
Into each other
With such ferocity
To eat
Every morsel
Of sensuous love
Moving in every shape
Every dance
Trying to find
Movements
That don't even exist
Arms entwined
Lips locked
The bodies immersed
In eternal embrace
Not letting go of each other
Not letting the moment end.

It is the last night
The final night
When bodies
Become
One soul

An inseparable soul
Engulfed in each other
Moving gently
And harshly
Thrusting
Receding
Plunging
Trying to find openings
That do not even exist
Quivering with passion
The crescendo of music
Reaching its peak
'Til it erupted
To the joys of the soul
To the joy of the gods
Into a sweet bliss
Creating
A mark on our souls
For in one moment
We merged into each other
Inseparable forever
All inhibitions gone

We were one
Completely one
One soul
That would
Forever
Remain one
As our juices
Flow into each other
To remain there
As part of our blood
To become one
Throughout eternity
Entwined forever

As the night ends
The rays of the sun
Create dawn
The bodies spent
Still intertwined
Lying in
A state of meditation
Peaceful and at bliss.

We have become one
Our hearts are now one
Our sensations are one.

We part
But cannot part
Our senses have become one
Our scents have become one
We are now one
Throughout this life
And throughout eternity
It is the last night
It is the feast of love
We have eating everything
We are full and satisfied
And in God's Hand
It is truly
The love feast.

THE FEAST OF LOVE

There comes a day
In one's life
When love
Becomes a delicacy
It takes over the entire body
You feel love
From head to toe
Full of emotions
Passion and sensuousness
It oozes out of the body
It creates a feast
That will be remembered
Forever.

That one evening
That one night
That lasts forever
It is
The feast of love
The feast to remember

It starts with gentle music
Soft candles
With the scent of
Flowers and incense
Aromating the atmosphere.

The slow dance
The tender touching of bodies
Arms slowly encircling
Each other
The breast
Against the chest

The thighs
Against thighs
The tender caressing
Of backs
The soft kisses
On the cheeks
As passions rise
The lips touch
Creating a tingle
The reverberates
Throughout the body
The embrace tightens
The mouths open
Sensing the scent
Of tongues
As they explore
Each other's mouths
The bodies grinding
Getting hard and moist
As hands roam
Pulling each other
Trying to break
The membrane
Of clothing
Wanting to feel
Flesh
As clothes shed
From top to bottom
The touch of nipples
On chest
Sends lightening
Throughout the body
The hardness
Cupped by thighs

The tip
Rubbing the moistness
As passions grow
The bodies
Tumble to the floor
'Til in an embrace
Bodies locked
As senses erupt
The hands
Spread all over the body
The tongues
Wanting to taste
Every morsel of flesh
Sucking
Ears, neck
Chest, breast
Nipples
Biting and sucking
As mouths
Hungrily travel down
Sucking and eating
The life-givers
As bodies
Go into convulsions
The feast has begun
As we suck
Every juice out of each other
But the hunger
Has just begun
The body wants more
As tongues
Explore every crevice
Trying to suck
Every oyster
Wrapped a pearl

The inflamed bodies
The interlocked tongues
As mouths make
Love to each other
The tongues
Locked in sweet embrace
The bodies
Grinding rhythmically
To find spaces
That don't exist
And naturally
The bodies find
The depths
Which are their homes
Places to nest
And find peace
The main course is here
The love smells
The aroma
The savoring of taste
The bodies know
It is the last night
A night when
Every inhibition
Is thrown away
The bodies want
To merge with
Each other
Become one
Forever.

The bodies are
Fully immersed
Moving and pushing
Shoving and pulling

As they find
Holes
That will give them peace
A home
Where they can
Lie in quietness
Completely
Oblivious of the world
But the passions
Are aroused
The bodies want
To move
But love
Wants to rest
As bodies turn
In different directions
Top to bottom
Bottom to bottom
Top to top
Plunging and exploring
Eating and sucking
'Til the right
Food is sought.

The devouring begins
The gorging begins
You eat, you eat
You plunge and plunge
The bodies
Engorged, immersed
As passions erupt
The embrace tightens
The bodies intertwine
And shudder with joy
As all that we have
Is now satisfied.

But the feast
Does not end
The sensations
Have become inflamed passions
As love, passion and senses
Form their own juice
A new scent
A new aroma
That is us
As evening becomes night
As night goes on
Not wanting the dawn to come
The bodies exhausted
And alive
Not giving up moving
Wanting to squirt
Whatever is still left
The romance
Does not want to extricate
The hunger
Is not over
The feast of love
Goes on
As bodies
Refuse to part
There is still
Life left
The passions are aroused
This time
It is tender
Gentle and loving
Savoring the taste
Smelling the aroma

Inciting emotions
That just don't
Want to give up
But consume
Every food
That left untouched
The exhausted bodies
Find new positions
New movements
Smelling new juices
The earth underneath
Shuddering
Getting heated
As lava boils
Ready to erupt
As bodies squirt
Over each other
Lunge into each other
Erupting with hotness
Every fluid that existed
'Til there is nothing
To come out
The feast is over
Bodies satisfied
Love fulfilled
It is truly
A feast of love.

THE WORLD IN MY ARMS

When I hold you
I feel the world
In my embrace
As if
What I wanted
In this life
Was with me
In me
I am complete
Devoid of any desire
For all desires
Fulfilled
Lay in my arms
Content and peaceful
Touching the soul
That unites us
Into a universe
Of our own
With all its beauty
Serenity and calmness
Mystery and love
When I have you
In my arms.

THE PASSION

The passion
Tempered with love
Arouses senses
That intoxicates us
And transports us
Into a world
That just belongs to us
When we become the world
Holding and touching
Embracing and caressing
The bodies
Singing with delight
As they explore each other
Trying to find spaces
Where no spaces exist
Creating new aliveness
Of wonders and feelings
That only passion can seek
Full of love
To embrace love
With its might
And crush it
Into one world
Of love and passion

THE TOUCH

The gentle touch
Caressing
Tingling of fingers
Twining of fingers
Clasping of hands
Shudders a sensation
That vibrates
The entire body
Sending feelings
That arouse emotions
To hold you
To embrace you
Gently but firmly
Letting bodies touch
And explore each other
Seeking unity of emotions
Engulfing passions
To fire our bodies
Into an eternal fire
Of merging souls

It was just a beginning
It was just a touch
The touch

THE SHEETS

The sheets
If they could talk
They will tell
Stories
About our love
And our lovemaking
How we groped
And explored
Each other
From top to bottom
And everything
In between

The lying down
Feeling the softness of the sheets
The ruffling movements
The shuffling bodies
Reaching for each other
Turning over on our sides
Facing each other
Adjusting our arms
Our bodies
'Til we are body locked
In an embrace
That places our lips
Next to each other
Hungrily searching for each other

They kiss
They lock in an eternal embrace
Exploring

Each other's wet mouths
Tongues lashing out
To elicit
Every sweet nectar

Absorbing flavors
Sweet and godly
Probing its depths
To reach the mind
To tell you
I am yours
You are mine

I want you
You want me

As our arms tighten around us
Pulling us closer
'Til there is no air
Between us
Just two bodies
Glued to each other
Penetrating
Each other's depths
To find comfort
That lies within us

Our bodies struggle
Grapple
Twist and turn
'Til we are locked from top to bottom
In each other
Trying to release the tension
Searching for serenity
That lies within us

Creating movements
Like the rhythms of the waves
Rising to meet the next wave
Undulating like a pendulum
Rocking to and forth
Waiting for the big wave
Its onslaught
Its fury
Its passion
Matching it
With determined force
To tear apart the water
With our own fury, passion and love

The words come in spurts
Whispering
Everlasting love
As our bodies
Continue
Intertwining
Tightening our hold
To never let it go

Movements
Synchronizing
With our breaths
Never separating our mouths
Never leaving our interlocked thighs
Our bodies inside each other
Releasing the nectar of life
That fills both of us
In a sweep

Just as Tsunami hits us
With gigantic force
Expending our energies
Into each other
Washing us
Devoid of life
Listless, spent
Contented, peaceful
Unified, one, immersed, souled
Sharing specks of life
That may ignite
Other life

The waves
Retreating
Leaving us
Together and one
Still immersed and joined
To rest in each other's arms
Quietly and gently
Fulfilled and filled

On the sheets

I REMEMBER YOU

I remember you,
> When you are not there.

I remember you,
> When I feel your presence.

I remember you,
> When your thoughts touch mine.

I remember you,
> When I feel your eyes gaze into me.

I remember you,
> When I feel your tenderness.

I remember you,
> When I feel your embrace.

I remember you,
> When I think of your world.

I remember you,
> When I want to share happiness.

I remember you,
> When I want to share my pain.

I remember you,
> When there is no one there for me.

I remember you,
> When life just wants you.

I remember you,
> When the world is just you.

That is,
I remember you,
> All the time.

CONTENTMENT

I feel contented
Now that I am in love.
Love with someone
That enlivens you
That brings life to you,
Knowing that life
Is just a memory of today.

Today determines the future
The future, that is unknown
We are there, yet not there,
Each second moves us in the future
Leaving the past behind.

Past that was not a past
Past that I am not proud of
But, the future opens me,
Scares me, yet
Future is where I must live
For future is where my life is
In future lies my happiness
And, in future, lies my salvation.

The past came and went
Future is where I belong.
The love opens the future
A place where I bloom
And find contentment.

It is my life
Love is my life
And in love
I find life
And contentment.

THE MOMENT

The moment
When the flow of emotions
Sparks between two hearts
Igniting a passion
That engulfs the mind and body.

When that happens,
We don't know
It just happens
We don't feel.

At that moment
When fate entwines us
Creating a new bond
Of love, feelings and warmth
That forever breaks all barriers
And makes us one soul
That then journeys together
To create a new moment
That fills our lives and bodies
With eternal love
And that is
The moment.

YES, I LOVE YOU

Yes, I love you!
The words I have spoken
To you many times,
Sometimes knowingly
Sometimes unknowingly
But, every time
I meant it.

Love is such a strong force
That creates emotions
We didn't know we had
Some good, some bad.
Some we control,
Some we don't.

Love brings us together
Pulls us apart
For that is love
A part of life
That cannot change.
Yes, I love you.

TOGETHER YET APART

I see you in my heart
The throbbing of life
In my veins
Is you
For you are my life
I feel you in me
And then I look around
And don't see you
I am alone
With no one to touch
Just a memory of a love
Within me
But, no one to hold
We are together through eternity
But apart forever.

THE EMPTY BED

I reach across the bed
Searching for you
It is middle of the night
It is cold and lonely
I search for warmth
A touch
Just to feel
That there is you
There on the other side of the bed
But, the space is empty
A cold mattress
I grope
Hands and fingers
Hoping for a body
'Til it dawns on me
That I am alone in bed
I cry silently
Lamenting at an empty bed.

THE LOVE OF MY LIFE

The love of my life
Is missing
In flesh and touch
But remains in my heart
As a love
Carved in my heart
And that is
The love of my life.

TOGETHER YET ALONE

Somewhere out there
Is a person I love
She knows I love her
I know she loves me
Our hearts are one
We are together
But alone
The distance between us
Is too far
That cannot be overcome
But longings and desires
Brings us together
Yet separates us
We are together
In one sense
But may remain
Apart forever.

ABOUT THE AUTHOR

Dan Khanna considers himself a traveler through life enjoying an adventurous journey.

Dan was born in New Delhi, India. After he completed high school at St. Columbus High School, Dan left India striking out for California via short stays in London, Montreal and Milwaukee, Wisconsin. Although his dream was to pursue a career in the arts, acting, music, and writing, a quirk of fate placed him in engineering college and pursuing a business management career, in which he excelled. Dan completed an undergraduate program in engineering, and a Master and Doctorate in Business Administration.

Dan worked in Silicon Valley's high technology firms and was a CEO and founder of several firms. He changed careers to be a professor. Now, he again is pursuing his dream in creative endeavors.

Dan is the quintessential Renaissance Man, whose interests span the gamut of the arts, sciences, history, social and political studies, classics and philosophy. His search for knowledge began in his early life where his father was the Chief Education Officer of Delhi and his mother was a Sanskrit scholar. Dan speaks English, Hindi, Urdu, Punjabi, and Gujarati.

As a child, Dan read voraciously, particularly enjoying novels, such as Sherlock Holmes, Agatha Christie, Earl Stanley Gardener, Ian Fleming's James Bond series and classic works of Shakespeare, Tolstoy, Dickens, Oscar Wilde, Thomas Hardy, and other writers. He was very interested in poetry and read English poems of Browning, Keats, Milton, Tennyson, and Frost, as well as, other poets, while mastering Urdu poetry. His intellectual interests including studying Western and Eastern philosophers, especially Socrates, from whom he learned questioning methodology employed in his research, lectures and seminars.

During his parochial education, Dan was interested in various sports: cricket, soccer and field hockey. His love for the arts and music was honed to a level that he performed in plays, movies and solo concerts.

Dan's present journey is devoted to creative arts and activities, primarily writing poetry, fiction and non-fiction books and plays, while continuing to acquire knowledge of diverse subjects. He has published one book and has written over twelve hundred poems comprising nineteen books to date. Dan has several non-fiction and fiction books in development.

www.ingramcontent.com/pod-product-compliance
Lightning Source LLC
Chambersburg PA
CBHW071415040426
42444CB00009B/2264